Police Officers

Laura K. Murray

seedlings

CREATIVE EDUCATION • CREATIVE PAPERBACKS

Published by Creative Education and Creative Paperbacks
P.O. Box 227, Mankato, Minnesota 56002
Creative Education and Creative Paperbacks
are imprints of The Creative Company
www.thecreativecompany.us

Design by Ellen Huber
Production by Grant Gould
Art direction by Rita Marshall
Printed in the United States of America

Photographs by Agefotostock (DreamPictures), Alamy
(Juniors /Bildarchiv GmbH, Elliot Nichol, John Roman),
Dreamstime (Seanlockephotography), Getty (DNY59,
inhauscreative, kali9, Joe Raedle, JOEL SAGET, Jeremy
Woodhouse), iStock (AlexRaths, Juanmonino, RichLegg),
Shutterstock (Katrina Brown, Jun3, Photo Spirit, Lisa F.
Young)

ISBN 9781640264151 (library binding)
ISBN 9781628329483 (paperback)
ISBN 9781640005792 (eBook)

LCCN 2020907031

TABLE OF CONTENTS

Hello, police officers!

Police officers help in an emergency. They race to help. They also stop people who break the law.

Officers work at a police station.

They drive
police cars, too.

Some ride motorcycles or bikes.

They ride horses. Others ride in helicopters or boats.

K-9 officers work with police dogs. The dogs sniff out danger.

They find
lost people.

A police officer
wears a uniform.
It has a badge.

A vest keeps the officer safe. A belt holds tools.

Police officers listen to people in the community. They work together.

They try to make things better.

Thank you,

police officers!

Picture a Police Officer

hat

radio

uniform

badge

utility belt

21

Words to Know

emergency: important need for help

law: rules everyone must follow

uniform: a special set of clothing worn by all members of a group

Read More

Donner, Erica. *Police Station*.
Minneapolis: Jump!, 2018.

Leaf, Christina. *Police Officers*.
Minneapolis: Bellwether Media, 2018.

Websites

Police Coloring Pages
http://www.supercoloring.com/coloring-pages/tags/police

The Sheriff's Office
https://www.pbs.org/video/kidvision-vpk-sheriffs-office

Index